D1514520

28-Day Wall Pilates Challenge

The Ultimate Guide to Wall Pilates Workouts Suitable For Women, Seniors and Beginners

Michael Hanchett

Copyright © Michael Hanchett 2023

Table of Content

Other Books By the Author

Wall Pilates for Seniors

28-Day Wall Pilates Challenge

Introduction

I grew up in a family where exercise was a big part of our daily lives, thanks to my father, a trainer and fitness enthusiast. I remember my mom having a bad backache that won't just go away. Eventually, my dad came home one day and told us he had come across a new exercise routine to help my mom. The name of the exercise was wall *Pilates,* and it was new to us even though we were fitness buffs. My mom started engaging in this new exercise routine, and soon enough, she complained less about the pesky backache until it eventually disappeared. Wall Pilates as an exercise has been around for almost a century, and while it wasn't well known like Yoga, wall Pilates recently started to gain traction and is beginning to see more devotees. The exercise was founded by a man called Joseph Pilates around the early parts of the 20th century. This exercise was used for body conditioning and also a way for dancers who got injured to make a recovery. Due to the stressful repetitive routines that many dancers go through, they are often prone to injuries and muscle problems. However, wall Pilates helped these dancers make a recovery. Down the line, it was discovered that exercise is also beneficial for everyone.

The movements involved in wall Pilates focus on activating the core through abdominal curls and toe taps. It also improves the body through repeated leg extension movements. If this exercise is so great, it must have some benefits. Yes, it does! Wall Pilates has preventative and therapeutic benefits. With this exercise, a person's muscles are isolated and relaxed simultaneously. The exercise has also given its users core strength and breath control. Also, one of the benefits of this exercise is that it improves your posture and helps you walk straighter. So, if you've been struggling with having a better posture, wall Pilates may just be what you need. One more benefit of this exercise, before I tell you about the 28-day wall Pilates exercise plan that will help you live a healthier life. Wall Pilates also helps your muscles have more endurance, which is very helpful as we age. Thanks to its slow, controlled movements, this exercise will help you gain muscular endurance.

Now that we know what Wall Pilates exercise is all about and how it can benefit you, allow me to introduce you to a 28-day wall Pilates exercise plan. The concept is simple. For the next 28 days, I will take you through a series of well-tailored wall Pilates exercises, and each day is a step up from the previous day. The exercises will last 5-10 minutes, and each new exercise will build on the former. Some of the routines in the 28 days plan include supported roll downs, side leg swings, active calf stretch, and more. Engaging in wall Pilates will aid physical rehabilitation, improve muscular endurance and make you more flexible!

In this book, you will get a tremendous 28-day plan tailored just for you. What's better? We don't just talk about the daily exercises without giving you something to visualize. So, you can expect pictures of each of the daily exercises. We'd also modify the exercises so beginners and the physically challenged can benefit. Great, right? I know! The content of this book includes the benefits of wall Pilates and daily exercise routines that build upon the previous week's workouts. You will also need some materials before you start; I will discuss them in the first chapter. Read on!

Chapter 1

Getting Started

Now that we know what wall Pilates is and how it can benefit those who practice it, it is time for us to begin preparing for the 28-Day-Wall Pilates-Challenge journey, and on this journey, there are a few things that we must have. If you have exercised before, you know some basic things you need, such as a mat, waist trainer, etc. This also applies to wall Pilates. Below are some of the things you'll need before starting wall Pilates

1. Pilates Mat

Of course, we just had to start with the mat because it is one the most straightforward Pilates kits to purchase. It won't bore a hole in your pocket and can be easily found in most fitness stores. Wall Pilates mats are designed to be thicker than the mat used in Yoga. Why are wall Pilates mats thicker? Well, we are glad you asked. The answer is relatively straightforward; wall Pilates mats are designed to be wider so that your joints, hands, and spine are protected as you work out. It ensures that your joints are cushioned throughout the exercises. This also helps you to carry out the exercises for a long time because your joints won't get fatigued during the workout.

You can also use the exercise mat you use for other exercises as a Pilates exercise mat. However, check your mat's thickness before using it for wall Pilates. Many exercises that are done during wall Pilates will require that you press your hand or some part of your body down on the mat. This is why you must have a thick mat, so your hands and knees don't feel sore during the wall

Pilates. The good news about this wall Pilates mat is that it can be used for almost all exercises.

2. Comfortable Clothes

Gotten your wall Pilates mat yet? If you have, great! Let us now see what type of clothes you need to wear for your exercise. The same clothes you wear to do other exercises, such as Yoga, also apply to wall Pilates. But, for those who don't know, I'd talk about the clothes that should be used when engaging in wall Pilates exercises.

Whether you are doing your wall Pilates at home or doing it in a class, avoid wearing baggy clothes. Baggy clothes won't allow you or the instructor to see your form, which is crucial in any exercise. If you don't get the form right, your exercise is as good as useless. You should wear a fitted workout top to allow you and the instructor to see and analyze your body form and movement. We also advise choosing a tank top that helps your limbs and rib cage to be seen. You must also ensure the clothes are stretchable to make your stretches comfortable. Remember that wall Pilates exercises require you to lie on a mat often. So, it is a good idea for you to avoid clothes that tie at the back to save yourself discomfort. Clothes with flat seams are great because they will eliminate extra friction during your workout.

Now, for the leggings. We should not be saying this, but don't wear jeans for a workout! Instead, wear leggings that allow you to stretch comfortably. It is a good idea to pick form-fitting leggings, but you can also opt for shorts. If you're going to choose shorts, ensure that they are fitted. You don't want to be flashing your instructor during class. We understand that some people may not feel comfortable wearing leggings; if that is you, you can opt for compression shorts which should go underneath your gym shorts. After wearing your shorts, do some lunges to see if they fit well. Besides flashing your instructor during class, you don't want your shorts riding up, even if you do wall Pilates at home.

When choosing to clothe for wall Pilates, ensure that you also pick breathable fabrics. You can cool down quickly during your workout by selecting a moisture-wicking material. These shirts can draw away moisture from your skin as you exercise. Moisture-wicking materials allow you to stay cool and sweat-free as you exercise. Moisture-wicking fabrics are also ideal for wall Pilates because they are form-fitting and lightweight. If, like us, you like to sweat it out during your workouts, then wear a cloth made with hemp or cotton material. The sports bra for your wall Pilates has to be a low-impact one. While wall Pilates isn't a high-intensity workout, your chest must be well-supported as you work out. If you ignore wearing a bra during your exercise, you risk straining your breast alignment, which can lead to tissue damage. You don't want that.

Also, wear grippy socks during your wall Pilates workout. This is because these socks will prevent slippage. If you have sweaty feet, use a sock that allows more ventilation. Finally, if you have long hair, you should tie it with a hair tie. You don't want hair getting into your face as you exercise. If you will do your wall Pilates in a class, carry extra hair ties in case someone else needs them.

3. Pilates Ring

To get the best out of your wall Pilates exercises, you may also need a Pilates ring. The Pilates ring helps to improve your balance during your workout. The Pilates rings usually come with two padded handles that can be comfortably gripped using the ankles, thighs, etc. These rings are great for toning body parts such as arms, chests, etc.

4. Sturdy Wall

You can't do wall Pilates without a wall. That is pretty obvious. So, choose a dedicated wall for your programs. The wall has to be strong and allows you to balance your weight on it. You also need to get a glove. This is to avoid staining your wall during your exercise. You will place your hands on the wall; a glove can help ensure you don't leave any unsightly hand marks on your wall.

5. Pilates Ball

Finally, let us talk about the Pilates ball. You can choose the ball you want based on its shape or size. The stability ball, called the Swiss ball, is used when targeting specific parts of your body. The Swiss ball is also helpful for improving balance and increasing flexibility. It is also beneficial for activating core strength.

6. Water Bottle

For the 28-day wall Pilates plan, you will also need to get a water bottle in handy. Even though wall Pilates isn't a very tasking exercise, you are bound to sweat, leading to dehydration of your body. So, get a good water bottle and store water that will be used as you exercise. It would help if you went for a water bottle that will preserve the temperature of what you put in it, preferably water. I enjoy drinking cold water when doing my wall Pilates, but it's just my preference. Keep your water intake low during the wall Pilates workout programs. You don't want a belly full of water as you exercise because it will make you heavy. Small sips in between each exercise are recommended.

Wall Pilates Safety Tips

Safety is paramount during any exercise. We once had a student who didn't adhere to the safety tips we laid down during our classes. This student was too eager to jump into the exercises and start without any warm-up. Of course, this inevitably leads to muscle pulls and injuries. The significance of safety during any fitness regimen cannot be overstated. Check out some safety tips below.

- **Warm Up**

Any instructor that tells you to jump into any exercise without a proper warm-up is a quack, and you should ditch them fast. Warm-up is crucial to any exercise. While wall Pilates is a mental activity, it is also a physical training program. It will help if you spend much time centering yourself and preparing your mind and body for the exercises. Great warm-up exercises include imprinting and pelvic curls. One of the benefits of a good warm-up is the fact that it will raise your body temperature. When your body's temperature gets raised, it helps your body muscles. When your body muscle temperature increases, more oxygen will be available for your muscles. This would allow you to perform more exercises efficiently. A good warm-up will also help your heart prepare, and you won't be too stressed when you start working out.

You don't want to start your wall Pilates exercise and get injured. When you warm up, your muscle elasticity improves and allows for efficient cooling. This means you have less chance of hurting yourself by accident.

When you jump straight into a workout without adequate preparation, it can mess you up mentally. It is essential to warm up for wall Pilates because wall Pilates is both mental and physical. Also, without warming up well, you'd easily quit when the exercise gets too tricky because you aren't mentally prepared. We use my warm-up to prepare for what we are about to do. Warm-up exercises should also be performed to improve flexibility. In the long and short term, warm-ups will enhance blood flow to your muscles and assist your body in becoming more flexible.

- **Head Placement**

You must note that your head will get heavy when you attempt to do wall Pilates at home. This is why the way you place your head is essential. When you begin doing wall Pilates, you must keep your head down significantly if you suffer from neck or back problems. If you establish a strong core, it will be easy for you to maneuver your head and neck without strain.

One thing I do is think of the neck and head as extensions of my spine. When doing a wall Pilates exercise, lift your head if you're on your stomach to reduce the strain on your neck.

- **Keep Reps Controlled and Low**

Another safety tip when doing your wall Pilates is to control your reps. A controlled rep will maximize the results of your cuts and sculpting. I know there is a temptation for many people to try and get in as many reps as possible when doing exercises. However, the advantage of controlled reps is that your form will not be compromised. Too many reps can compromise your form and may even lead to injuries.

- **Protect Your Neck and Spine**

It would help if you protected your neck and spine during wall Pilates exercises. A good neck roll is recommended for head support. If you are engaging in an exercise requiring you to lift your legs above your head, don't use a pillow under your neck, as it may lead to neck strains. If you are suffering from back pain, skip any wall Pilates exercise where you'd need to roll. You can replace rolling exercises with balance exercises. Always limit the number of reps you perform, and always rest between workouts if you have heart or respiratory issues.

Essential Wall Pilates Breathing Techniques

When exercising, it is essential to breathe right. If you don't breathe correctly during your exercises, you stand the chance of not getting the best out of your exercise or, worse, run the risk of injury. Below are some great breathing techniques you can implement during wall Pilates workouts.

- **Lateral Breathing**

The lateral expansion of the rib is where the emphasis is laid during lateral breathing. The ribs are laterally expanded during the exercise, while an inward pull of the deep abdominal muscles is maintained during breathing in and out. Lateral breathing is in stark contrast to diaphragmatic breathing, which encourages lowering the diaphragm when breathing in. So, why should one use lateral breathing during wall Pilates exercise? Lateral breathing is encouraged during wall Pilates because it helps maintain abdominal contraction, stabilizing your core. When your core is stable during wall Pilates exercise, your body will be protected and perform well. Keep in mind that we are not discouraging diaphragmatic breathing during wall Pilates. However, we are saying that lateral breathing is the preferred and recommended mode during wall Pilates exercises.

During lateral breathing, you should keep your shoulders down as you breathe. Your shoulders should be relaxed. Don't raise your shoulders. You aren't doing it right if your shoulders are touching your ears. The neutral spine position is the correct positioning for your spine. Breathe in through your nose. Slowly. Ensure that the air you inhale is flowing through your chest and allow it to fill you up. You should feel your ribs expanding on all sides. Keep your stomach relaxed. Finally, exhale through your mouth, allowing your ribs to deflate. Congratulations! You've just done posterior lateral breathing.

- **Breathing Patterns**

During wall Pilates, there are patterns of breathing that are important for you to do. As an instructor, our students are encouraged to breathe in during one phase of the exercise and breathe out in the next phase. Breathing in and out in phases during an exercise is a very crucial part of the program, and here's why; When a person is doing an exercise that requires a lot of effort, there is a tendency for that person to want to hold their breath. However, when you hold your breath, you are creating too much muscle tension and a rise in blood pressure. When you exhale in the part of the exercise that requires a lot of effort, you can prevent that impulse that makes you want to hold your breath. Your deep abdominal muscles can also be activated when you exhale.

When you establish a breathing pattern during your wall Pilates exercise, you will notice that your exercise goes into a rhythm. One of the great things about wall Pilates and Pilates exercise is the fact that each of the exercises has a specific quality. Wall Pilates exercises are performed in a slow and smooth pattern. Then, others are done rapidly. The advantage of the different dynamics in wall Pilates exercises is that it simulates daily activities and creates variety for your workout.

- **Active Breathing**

This type of breathing can also be used during wall Pilates. For example, in exercises such as *hundred,* there is a forceful pushing out of breath in a percussive manner. The practitioner of the exercise will also purposefully contract their abdominal muscles. When doing *the hundreds,* a practitioner will draw breath using a percussive emphasis that highlights the external intercostal muscles.

Using active breathing during wall Pilates is based on individual preferences. However, if you are the type of person who workout with excess tension, you are encouraged to employ a softer mode of breathing. Some people use active breathing to infuse energy into their wall Pilates exercises. Some people also use active breathing to target specific muscles, activating them.

- **Diaphragmatic Deep Breathing**

When engaging in wall Pilates, it is essential to take advantage of every breath. The founder of Pilates, Joseph Pilates, believed that the blood needed to be boosted with oxygen which helps to purge the blood of any waste. He also wanted Pilates practitioners to inhale to oxygenate the blood and then do a full exhale to get rid of stale air. Thanks to diaphragmatic breathing, we can achieve the aims of Joseph Pilates quickly. Learning how to do diaphragmatic breathing is essential in understanding the deeper types of breathing.

Diaphragmatic breathing isn't only applicable in Pilates but also in Yoga. This breathing style is also used for meditation and singing.

The diaphragm plays a significant role in human breathing. That is why when the diaphragm collapses, it is usually fatal for a person. When a person inhales, this dome-shaped muscle flattens downwards and contracts. This helps it to create a vacuum for sucking in air. When a person exhales, the diaphragm will return to its default shape, pushing out air from the body. In the next paragraph, I'll show you how to do diaphragmatic breathing.

First, you must lie on your back or go into a sitting position. Place a hand on your belly and another on your chest—the part where your heart is located. Now, breathe in through your nose. Remember that you have to send the air into your belly. Ensure that your gut is filled with air. Observe that the hand you rested on your belly will rise as your stomach fills with air.

Next, see if you can move the breath up into your chest. See if you can fill up the bottom parts of your lung and then ensure that you fill your lungs to the top. Ensure that your lungs are filled with air. Your throat should remain open. Now, you need to release the air. When removing the air, you should consider your body a vessel. Allow the air to go out of the vessel—your body—just as it will from a water bottle. Please don't force it; it should feel like a natural release of breath. Keep practicing diaphragmatic breathing until you are familiar with it.

You can't talk about any Pilates exercise without mentioning *The hundred.* The hundred can be a very intense workout, and we usually find our first-time students struggling to execute it. Using wall support is a great way to make *The Hundred* a bit easier. What are the benefits of this exercise? *The Hundreds* is a great way to warm up your abdominals and lungs. This exercise requires the practitioner to coordinate their breathing with body movements while simultaneously being graceful and strong. This exercise uses the lateral abdominal muscles while developing trunk stability.

Step 1

With your back on the ground, flatten your feet on your mat and keep your knees bent. Your feet should be kept flat. Ensure that the tips of your toe are touching the wall. Your toe touching the wall will keep your feet in the same line. This is important for alignment because your toes will be used to establish the symmetry of your hips and knees.

Step 2

Are you in the correct position, just as we described above? Let us go to the next step. From the position you are in now, move your arms up until they are at a 45 degrees angle. Your arms should be in the same line as your thighs. Now, lift your shoulder and neck off the mat slowly! Don't rush it. As you lift your shoulders and neck off the mat, ensure your upper abdominals contract.

Step 3

Next, pump your arms and inhale for five counts. Exhale at five counts. Repeat the motion you are currently doing for ten counts until it reaches 100 pumping counts. If it is too easy for you, you can level it up by lifting your legs into the air and keeping your feet on the wall, but this time, in a tabletop position. Place your shins in a way that is parallel to the ground. Also, ensure that your thighs are perpendicular to your shins while your feet are flat against the wall.

If you are a beginner or you have a physical disability that won't let your spine be in a neutral position as you do this exercise, you can bring your feet upwards toward the ceiling and then bend your knees. If your shoulders become very tense, lower your upper body to the mat. Finally, if your neck muscles feel tight and grippy, turn your head from side to side. When you turn your head to one side, inhale and when you turn it to the other side, exhale.

Day 2

Shoulder Bridge

For today's challenge, we will be doing *The Shoulder Bridge.* The shoulder bridge is a staple exercise in many Pilates classes thanks to its ability to improve posture and its practitioners' well-chiseled abs and glutes. There are different variations of the shoulder bridge, and we will explore the wall variation in this book. This exercise focuses on steady breathing and body stability. The shoulder bridge is an excellent exercise if you want more strength in your gluteal muscles, pelvic floor, and hamstrings.

Step 1

Start by laying on your back, bend your knees, and keep your feet flattened on the floor. Keep your feet wide apart while the tips of your toes touch the wall. Now pull your abdominals inward and upward while your back rests firmly on the mat.

Step 2

For the next step, you need to engage your glutes. While engaging your glutes, you must also keep curling the under of your hips while lifting them into the air. When you lift your hips, leave them there for four counts. You could keep them for longer but start with four counts. The duration of this exercise should be anywhere between 5-10 minutes.

If it is too easy for you and you wish to level it up, keep your feet flat against the wall on a tabletop while raising and lowering your hips. When you are leveling up, ensure that you consciously engage your abdominals, hamstrings, and glutes so that they support your spine. This would make the exercise much harder. Go ahead, knock yourself out.

If you are a beginner, you can try the elevated bridge by adding a ball at your feet. When you add the ball to your feet, place your heels on the top of the ball and raise your pelvis. The ball will make this exercise a bit easier for you.

Day 3

Arms Overhead

The arms overhead is a great exercise for those who wish to improve their chest, back, and shoulder strength. If you are the kind of person that is always hunched over work all day, this exercise is essential for you.

Step 1

Start by facing away from the wall in a standing position. Keep your feet a foot away from the wall, and then allow your shoulders, hips, and back to lean against the wall.

Step 2

Now lift your arms over your head. Ensure that your elbows are bent, then press back against the wall. Your fingertips should touch and create a diamond shape as you press. This motion may be complex for you, but you need to push until you can do it. For beginners, you can reduce the reps of this program if it's too difficult for you.

Step 3

For the third step, you need to push your arms upward. Then, straighten your arms till you can't stretch them any further. You must ensure that the wall and your elbows are still in contact. The tips of your finger should be kept together. We recommend that you repeat this ten times.

Day 4

Wall Squats

For the fourth day of our exercise, we will incorporate a little leg exercise called *The Wall Squat*. The wall squat is an excellent exercise if you are looking to target muscles in your core. Wall squats are also perfect for getting your lower body in shape. If you are among those who usually skip leg day when working out, the wall squat can be one of your leg-day routines.

Step 1

Now let us get into doing a few wall squats. Start by standing with your feet a foot away from the wall. Your hips, shoulders, and back should lean against the wall. Next, keep your arms at your side. The palm of your hand should face the wall.

Step 2

For the next step, bend your knees and slide down the wall slowly. Don't rush it. Remember I told you that the effectiveness of your workout isn't in speed or how many reps you can get in, but in how much impact each rep makes in your body. The goal of sliding down the wall is to slide down to a point where your thighs are parallel to the floor. As you slide down the wall, your arms should go forward until they parallel the floor. Go ahead, try it!

Step 3

Now straighten back your legs to your standing position. As you straighten your legs, your arms should come down and return to your sides. Stay in rhythm and go down for four counts. Hold your position for four counts, and when you come up, hold for another ten counts. Do this for six or ten reps. Don't hold your position until you are fatigued. The goal of this wall Pilates exercise isn't for you to hold until exhaustion. Instead, the goal is for your glutes, quads, hamstrings, inner thighs, etc., to be worked out. Enough talk; now get into position and start!

A beginner modification for this exercise is keeping your knees from moving inwards and touching one another. This would ensure you don't go too deep in the sitting position. Also, for starters, you don't need to go too down when you can go halfway and come back up. It may also be more comfortable if you place a ball between your back and the wall.

You can also significantly decrease the intensity of the wall squat by aiming for a 45 degrees angle rather than a 90-degree angle. When you do a 45-degree angle, you will notice that a bit of pressure is taken off your knees, and the strain on your quads will be lightened. You can also make this easier by holding your position for much less and gradually increasing the hold.

Day 5

Wall Stretch

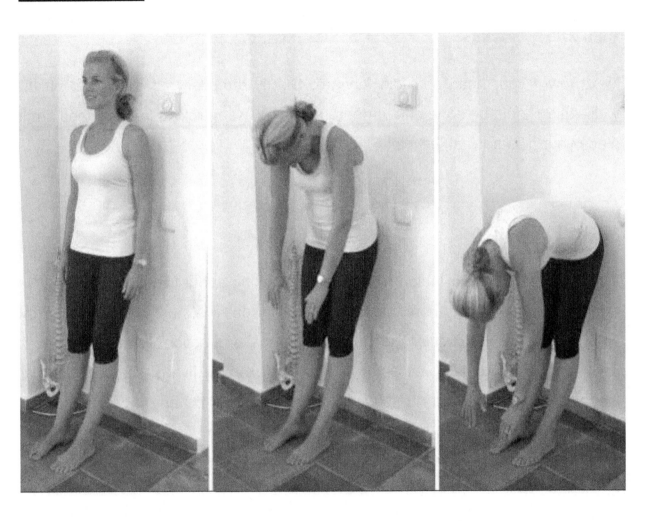

The Pilates wall stretch is a fantastic back and shoulder exercise. This workout is beneficial for those who experience back issues. Moreover, it can serve as a warm-down. For those who don't know what a warm-down is, it is an exercise that is done after other, more rigorous workouts. However, I recommend incorporating the Pilates wall stretch into your routine. For the fifth day of our wall Pilates challenge, we will do the wall stretch. Let us begin.

Step 1

Start by standing in a way that keeps your feet about a foot and a half away from the tower(wall). Your foot should be facing out. Next, lean against the wall using your hips, shoulders, and back.

Step 2

Next, lower your head and fold forward. Gently remove your shoulders off the wall—this should be done one vertebra at a time. Keep rolling forward, and firmly place your hips against the wall.

Step 3

While maintaining your folded position, start making about five circles using your arm as you move away from the center. Again, don't rush it. Take it slowly. Now stop and repeat the circular motion in the opposite direction. Next, you need to rise back up using the same pathway. Do this exercise five or six times in total. Remember that this is a stretch, and there shouldn't be any significant stress throughout this exercise. If you are feeling any tension, you aren't doing it right. This exercise aims to let your shoulders hang as you press your lower back against the wall.

As a beginner, you can make this exercise much easier for you by going down as far as you can. If you aren't comfortable going down all the way, you can go halfway.

Chapter 3

Days 6-10

Y ou are welcome to day 6! If you've successfully done the exercises from day 1-5, you should be feeling your body muscles getting stronger. Let us quickly start with the exercise(s) for day 6.

Day 6

Standing Hip Opener

The standing hip opener is usually used as a stretch. It is perfect for releasing hip tension and works well as a pain reliever. Follow the steps below to do a standing hip opener quickly.

Step 1

Begin by standing next to the wall. Place one hand on the wall.

Step 2

For this step, raise your thighs as high as you can. Ensure that your pelvis is level and square to the front.

Step 3

Now you have to place your inside hand on your raised thigh. This would serve as a support. Go ahead and press the leg that you raised into your hand and exhale as you open your legs to the side.

Step 4

Proceed to hold your breath for one second. Next, inhale and release your leg back to the starting position. Now, repeat this on the other side.

For beginners, please don't raise your legs too high so that this exercise doesn't become too difficult for you.

Side Leg Swing

The side leg swing stretches your calf, hamstrings, groins, and quadriceps. It will strengthen and give your arms some tone. The side leg swing will also give your upper body symmetry and help improve your posture. One of the added benefits of the legs swings is that it creates a pumping mechanism that allows fluid to flow in and out of the joints. It also stimulates blood flow around the surrounding tissue, improving flexibility in the joint capsule.

Step 1

Just like the other exercises in this book, you need to start by standing next to a wall. To give your body more support, place a hand on the wall.

Step 2

Next, raise your legs as high as you can. Ensure that your pelvis level is kept in a square shape to the front of your body.

Step 3

For this step, you have to swing your leg to the side while raising it high. However, it would help if you kept your pelvic level while raising your legs.

Step 4

Now you need to reverse your motion and swing your leg back to the position you started. Finally, repeat on the other side.

If you are a beginner or have a physical disability, you don't need to raise your legs too high. Just raise it to the level you are comfortable with, but as you proceed with the exercise, you can gradually lift your legs higher.

Day 7

Active Calf Stretch

If you have tightness in the calf, this exercise is what you'd need. Perhaps you are an athlete, and you are battling with tightness in your calf; all you have to do is perform a couple of active calf stretches, and you'd start to feel some relief of tension in your muscles. A good calf stretch will stretch your muscles and increase blood flow to the tight area. This exercise will increase your short-term range of motion and allow you to perform deeper stretches and exercises. For example, if you are to complete the wall squat, which we did on day 4, you'd need to do active calf stretches.

Step 1

For the first step, stand close to a wall and place your palm flat against the wall. When your palm is flat against the wall, ensure your shoulders aren't lifted.

Step 2

Now proceed to move your left leg two feet backward. Keep your heel firmly on the ground.

Step 3

For the next step, you have to keep your left straight and then bend your right knee. Lean against the wall and maintain doing so until your calf starts to stretch. Hold your breath and release for the next calf.

Supported Semi Lunge

One of the reasons why we love the supported semi-lunge is the fact that it is a multi-joint exercise. The lower parts of your body will benefit from these supported semi-lunges. The muscles that benefit from the supported semi-lunge are the quads, hamstrings, calves, and glutes. When you engage in wall lunges, your hip flexors are stretched, and this can improve flexibility. Wall lunges prevent tightening that usually happens when you sit in a place for too long. Have you ever felt tight in your calf sitting for too long? Then engage in supported semi-lunges.

Step 1

With one hand placed against the wall, stand next to it.

Step 2

Next, move your left leg two feet backward with your left palm against the wall.

Step 3

While your heels are kept down, your knees should be bent while you lean your torso forward. Lean your torso forward until you notice your hamstrings stretching. Just as we did in the active wall stretch, you will need to hold your breath for a few seconds and release and repeat this exercise on the right side.

If you are a beginner, you can make this exercise easier by leaning gently for a start. Don't lean in too hard until you feel more comfortable.

Day 8

Standing Knee Raise

This exercise is great for activating your quadriceps, calves, and glutes. It also helps to improve the endurance levels of your muscles. If you engage in this exercise regularly, you will notice you are getting more balance and coordination in your glutes, calves, and quadriceps muscles. If you do this exercise at a high intensity, it will also significantly improve the power in your lower body.

Step 1

To begin this exercise, you must support your body with a hand placed on your wall. Next, you have to lift your core and lift your knees towards your chest.

Step 2

You must press your lower back into the wall while raising your knees. Hold your position for a few seconds, then repeat the exercise for the other knee.

If you have a disability that won't let you do this exercise exactly as we described, you can place two hands on the wall for more support. Also, don't raise your knees too high. Instead, lift your knees comfortably and gradually see if you can work it higher over time.

Wall DB Arm Raise

The wall dumbell arm raise is excellent if you are looking to strengthen your deltoids and your pectorals. The strength in your shoulders will also improve significantly the more you engage in this exercise. Your anterior deltoid is one of the target muscles for this exercise, and it also targets other muscles such as the lower trapezius, serratus anterior, biceps, and pectoralis major.

Step 1

Proceed to stand against the wall. Just like the name of this exercise implies, you'd need to use two dumbells in each hand. Your elbows should be kept bent at about 90 degrees.

Step 2

For the next step, you must brace up your core and raise your arms slowly. Raising your arms should be done slowly so that your muscles get the benefits of each rep. Until your arms are parallel to the floor, don't stop raising them.

Step 3

With your arms raised in a straight line, hold the position for a few seconds and slowly lower your arms down until they are straight against your body.

For beginners, we advise that you use a lighter dumbbell. The heavier the dumbell, the more difficult this exercise will be. It would help if you raised your arms until they were in a straight line. However, if you can't raise your arms as big as we recommend, you can extend them halfway for a start.

Day 9

Wall DB Arm Circles

Congratulations, we are on day 9 of our wall Pilates 28-day challenge. Today, we will be doing an exercise that is a step up to the wall dumbell arm raise, and it's called *The wall DB Arm Circles.* The wall DB arm is excellent for working out your core and giving your muscles a nice toned look. This exercise is also great for working on your upper back muscles. The wall DB arm circles can be considered an excellent full-body workout.

Step 1

This exercise starts when you stand against the wall holding light dumbells in each of your hands. Keep your elbows at 90 degrees.

Step 2

Now you need to proceed to brace your core and raise your arms. Your arms should be raised until they are in a straight line.

Step 3

Now hold that position (your arms in a straight line), and begin to trace circles in the air for about 15-30 seconds. The circles you are tracing should be small.

Step 4

If you started tracing the circles clockwise, trace them in an anticlockwise position for another 15-30 seconds.

Is this too hard for you? You can reduce the weights of the dumbbells and also reduce the duration. So, instead of 30 seconds, you can circle your arms for 10 seconds.

Chest Openers

The wall chest openers come in handy when you are looking to reduce tension in your shoulders. If you struggle with raising your shoulders, the wall chest opener can free your shoulders and allow you to quickly raise them. This exercise also aligns your head and body while reducing stress on your neck. The wall opener will stretch your chest and back muscles while giving strength to the postural muscles of your upper back.

Step 1

Like the other exercises in our 28-day wall Pilates workout challenge, the chest opener begins with you standing close to the wall. You have to stand with your back against the wall and keep your feet a small distance away from the wall. At shoulder height, place your palms flat on the wall.

Step 2

Now brace your core with your chest pressed against the wall. Next, slide your hands up the wall until your arms are fully stretched out on the wall. Finally, hold your breath for a few seconds and return to the starting position.

Day 10

Seated Opposite Toe Tap

The seated toe tap is one of the best exercises for stretching your hamstrings and calves. It has also been proven that this exercise can help reduce back pain, which is excellent for those recovering from a back injury. This exercise will help target the back of your body and stretch out any taut muscles in those parts. If you also want to improve your flexibility, this exercise is highly recommended!

Step 1

Your starting position for this exercise is sitting on the floor with your back against the wall. Your legs should be stretched out in front of you.

Step 2

Spread your legs out and press your lower back into the wall while bracing your core. Next, reach out until you can tap your left toe with your right hand. Reach out again and tap your right toes with your left hand. Repeat this motion for about 45 seconds.

If you are a beginner and can't reach your toes, try seeing how close you can get. Over time you can improve your reach. You can also make this exercise easier by not pressing your back too hard into the wall, allowing you to reach your toes easily.

Seated Spine Twist

Are you having problems with spinal mobility? Do you find it hard to maintain a good posture after sitting for a long time? What you need is a seated spine twist exercise. This exercise also helps tone your belly and massage your internal organs. You can perform this exercise as a warm-down or a main set. This exercise is very refreshing and relaxing at the same time. Sounds like something you want to try, right? Let's go.

Step 1

Sit down on the floor with your back against the wall. Like the seated opposite toe tap, your legs should be stretched before you. Your legs should be hip-width apart.

Step 2

Now you need to brace your core and then twist your torso to the right. As you turn your torso to the right, you must reach your left hand and touch the ground close to your right leg. Next, reverse the twist, stretch out your right hand, and feel the ground close to your left leg. Keep alternating sides for about 45 seconds.

If your hamstrings are too tight, place a small pillow under your hips. If your arms can't be stretched out, you can fold them over your chest.

Chapter 4

Days 11-15

Welcome to the eleventh day of our 28-day wall Pilates workout challenge. So far, we've done exercises that stretch the spine, improve core body strength, and even tone arm muscles. Keep reading as we take you through days eleven to fifteen.

Day 11

Scissors

The scissors wall Pilates exercise is a bit more advanced than most exercises we've discussed in this book. Don't be afraid; with some practice, you can get the scissors exercise done quickly. It is excellent for shoulder and pelvic stability. The scissors exercise focuses on your upper and lower abs, and when it is done right, it will engage your obliques, which makes it an excellent workout for the abs. This exercise stretches the hamstrings and the hip muscles.

Step 1

Lay down on your mat with your hands stretched away from your body.

Step 2

It would help if you made sure that the lower parts of your buttocks were touching the wall. Now, raise your legs and spread them out, as depicted in the illustration.

Step 3

Your feet should be bent with your toes pushed forward. Next, slowly raise your legs in a closing nothing until they touch each other. Lower them again until they are spread wide apart. Repeat the scissors motion for about 45 seconds or more.

If you are a beginner and find this difficult, don't stretch your legs too wide, and reduce exercise durations. If you are suffering from severe hip or back injuries, don't do this exercise.

Marching Bridges

Are you looking for an exercise that serves as a stepping stone to a single-leg bridge exercise? Then, the marching leg bridge is your best bet. This exercise can help open up the front of your hips and give you a good hip extension. If you are an athlete, you can't afford to underestimate this exercise because it will provide you with more power to push forward. The key to getting this exercise right is engaging your core muscles and improving each rep.

Step 1

Lay down on the floor and place both feet on the wall. The purpose of the wall is to act as a support "lift-off." You'd understand this better in the next step.

Step 2

Next, press against the wall with both feet and gently lift your lower back and butt off the floor. It would help to keep lifting until you are in a bridge position.

Step 3

Hold your position at the top. Now you have to lift each foot off the wall one after the other. It should feel as if you are marching. Lift them for ten counts. Remember that when performing the marching bridge, your pelvis should not sag, and your back should not get too arched.

Step 4

When you have made the marching motion, use your spine to roll down. Congratulations, you've done one rep. You still have nine more reps to go!

As a beginner, you may struggle to complete this challenge. If you are experiencing your knee falling across your body during the leg lifts, then try restacking in a 3-9 clock position and proceed to pull the leg out. Also, you can press your heels firmly on the floor, activating your back legs. This means that your feet will trigger the lifting movement instead of your spine—This tip is excellent if you are having problems lifting with your spine due to a back injury.

Day 12

Flamingo

Are you looking to get your body balanced? The flamingo exercise is your best bet. Standing on one leg is a great way to engage your core muscles while learning to balance yourself better. The flamingo exercise also engages your brain as you try to balance yourself, and it also burns more calories. So, how is the flamingo exercise done? Follow the steps below.

Step 1

It would help if you stood close to the wall sideways. Keep your left hip towards the wall.

Step 2

Next, bend your left knee and gently lift the foot behind you. Stand on your right leg but lift your left foot.

Step 3

For the next step, press your left knee into the wall. Do it with strength. Ensure that your pelvis and hips are squarely kept.

Step 4

Hold your current position for ten counts. If you aren't a beginner, you can hold on for longer. Repeat the exercise five times before switching over to the other side.

<u>Shoulder Shrugs</u>

Still, on the 11th day of our 28 days wall Pilates challenge, we will do the shoulder shrug. The shoulder shrug is handy for those engaged in a job where they need to bend over a desk for long periods. The posture of bending over a desk can take a toll on you quickly, resulting in back pain and bad body posture. The shoulder shrug is a great way to relieve back and shoulder tension. It aids in strengthening the shoulder and upper back muscles.

Step 1

Stand next to the wall but keep an arm and half-length distance. Keep your palms flattened against the wall.

Step 2

Have you engaged in push-ups before? If you have, then place your palms on the wall exactly the way you would typically do a push-up.

Step 3

With your arms kept straight, slide your shoulder blades until they are close to each other. Allow your body to shift forward.

Step 4

If your body is shifted forward, press away from the wall. As you push away from the wall, widen your shoulder blades.

If this exercise is too strenuous for you, reduce the reps and press gently away from the wall instead.

Forward Bend Back Lift

Let us take one more exercise for day 12. This exercise we are about to show you is the forward bend-back lift. The forward bend-back lift is a good exercise if you are looking to stretch your hips, calves, and hamstring. It also gives strength to the thighs and knees. If you are struggling with spine problems, this exercise has a great way of relieving spine tension. We also recommend this exercise because it is very soothing and nerve-calming.

Step 1

First, stand facing the wall.

Step 2

Start bending slowly until your upper body goes into a straight line position. Keep in mind that the back should not be raised while bending. Keep it flat.

Step 3

Your palm should be flat against the wall. Next, start raising your back legs slowly. The floor and your back leg should become parallel.

Step 4

Next, lower your back leg until it is halfway toward the floor. Don't lower it till it reaches this ground. Go ahead and perform 20 leg lifts on both legs.

If you are a beginner and having problems lifting your legs, you can ask a partner to assist in lifting your legs. Also, you can raise the leg halfway up. You can also start with ten leg lifts instead of the 20 we recommended.

Day 13

Forward Bend Side Lift

For this exercise, we will vary the forward bend-back lift. The only difference between the forward bend side lift and the forward bend back lift is the direction of your legs when lifted. This exercise is excellent for improving posture and strengthening your core muscles. It is also a great exercise for those who want to improve their endurance while adding strength to their thighs.

Step 1

Face the wall and bend down slowly. Your back should go into the same straight position we showed you in the previous exercise.

Step 2

Just as we mentioned in the previous exercise, your back should not be raised when bending. Maintaining a parallel position with the floor with your back is something you should strive towards.

Step 3

Your palms should also be kept flat on the wall.

Step 4

Begin to gently raise your back leg to the sides of your body. Your back leg should become parallel to the ground before you stop lifting. Your hips should also be kept level.

Step 5

You need to perform 20 side leg lifts with both your legs.

If you are finding it difficult to pull off this exercise, then don't raise your legs too high. Start with what is comfortable for you and gradually work your way up. You can also reduce the number of leg lifts you need to do.

Twist and Stretch

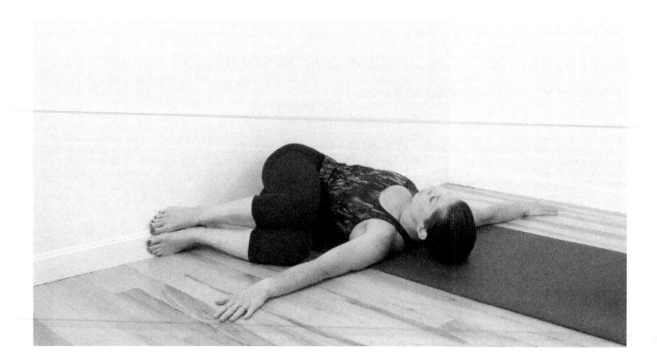

The following exercise for day 13 is the twist and stretch. This is an exercise we recommend for people struggling with spinal cord problems. When you engage in twists, your spine is stretched, settling into a deep position. Stretch exercises are known to help digestion and relax the practitioner's chest. The glutes, lower back, obliques, etc., are all stretched during the twist and stretch exercise.

Step 1

For a start, your legs should be up the wall. Your bottom should also be touching the wall.

Step 2

Your arms should be stretched on the sides and perpendicular to your torso.

Step 3

Proceed to bend your knees and let your feet flat on the wall.

Step 4

Next, gradually, move both your feet to the right till your right leg is now resting on the floor.

Step 5

While in the twist, ensure that you are breathing. It is essential to breathe so you don't begin to feel uncomfortable.

Step 6

Your upper back should be kept against the floor during this exercise. Count up to five using your breath. Slowly.

Step 7

Finally, switch sides and repeat this exercise.

Roll Up Into Bridge

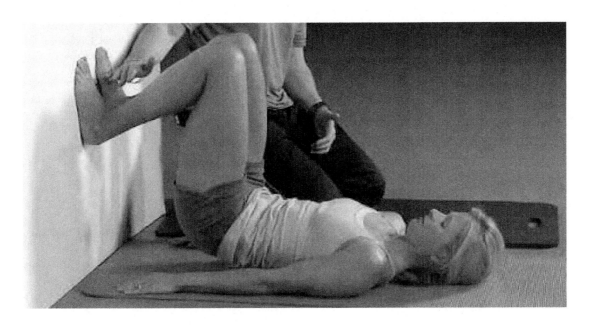

The roll-up into the bridge is an excellent exercise for strengthening the core. This exercise can also give your legs more power while hitting your abs and glutes.

Step 1

For your first step, you must sit facing the wall and keep your knees bent. Now, roll onto your back.

Step 2

Bend your knees at a 90-degree angle and straighten your elbows and pull your arms to your chest. Remember that this exercise will be highly effective if you can engage your core. Lift your hand as you roll. The roll should get you up to a sitting position. We advise that you roll up one vertebra at a time. Don't rush it.

Step 3

Rolling back to the ground, you must do it one vertebra at a time. Your arms should be rested on the ground and kept at your sides. Next, draw your pubic bone up to your tummy and press your feet against the wall as you enter a bridge position.

Step 4

Finally, scoop your pubic bone to your belly button, lower your hips, and back to the floor. Remember, one vertebra at a time.

If you are a beginner and can't use the roll to get into a bridge position, then don't do the roll. Just go into a bridge position by referring to our tutorials on the marching bridge.

Day 14

Kneeling Side Leg Lift

This exercise is an excellent way to build strength in your thighs and hip abductors. Some of the muscles this exercise makes are the medius and minimus. This exercise can be done lying down, but for our 28-day wall Pilates challenge, we will be doing it using a wall.

Step 1

Your left side should be towards the wall as you lower yourself into a high kneeling position. Place your left palm on the mat after lowering your left side. Your left palm should be directly placed beneath your shoulder. With your left foot placed against the floor, extend your left. You can rotate your knee for comfort.

Step 2

For the next step, you must lift your arm and place it above your head. You can place the tips of your finger on the wall and gently push it into the wall. Your pushing into the wall will activate your obliques and triceps.

Step 3

Your right toes should be pointed as you lift your right leg to hip length. Next, slowly lower your right leg, so your toes are just slightly over the ground. The ideal position for your toes should be hovering above the ground. Repeat this exercise while keeping your torso and leg aligned. Switch to your other leg after ten reps.

We usually advise beginners not to lift their legs too high for a start. Decreasing the lift on the leg will reduce the difficulty of this exercise. Also, a beginner can reduce the reps to 5 and gradually increase their reps as they get stronger.

Single Leg Bridge With Abduction

This exercise is excellent for those targeting their hamstrings, hip flexors, and lower back muscles. The single-leg bridge with an abductor is a good exercise for runners and people who lift weights. It is also beneficial to jumpers and people who sit down for extended periods. If you have injuries to your neck, back, or spine, it is essential that you seek advice from a doctor before engaging in this exercise.

Step 1

Start by getting into a sitting position. You should sit facing the wall and keep your knees bent.

Step 2

Roll onto your back one vertebra at a time and flatten your feet against the wall. Keep your feet hip-width apart. Just like our previous exercises, bend your knees at an angle of 90.

Step 3

For the third step, you will have to extend your right knee. However, while lifting your right knee, you must keep your left foot pressed against the wall. As you extend your right knee, raise your legs until they are straight up, pointing at the ceiling. Your toes should also be pointed at the ceiling.

Step 4

After completing the third step, you should draw your pubic bone towards your belly button. As you draw your pubic bone towards your belly button, you must press your left foot into the wall, lifting your hips as you go into a full bridge position.

Step 5

You have to engage your core muscles so that your pelvis will be kept level. While in the bridge position, slowly move your right leg out to the side—this is called abduction. It would help to draw your right leg out from your midline as far as possible without dropping your right hip.

Step 6

Finally, move your right leg back to your midline. Lower your hips and back gently to the floor. Do this exercise for ten reps and switch sides.

If you are a beginner, you can make this exercise easier by drawing out your legs not too far away from your midline. You can also reduce the reps before switching sides. If you are disabled or suffering back injury, talk to a doctor before engaging in the single-leg bridge with abduction.

Day 15

Side Plank With Rotation

One of the best ways to work the muscles along the side of your core is through the side plank with rotation. The muscles along the sides of your core help you bend and give your spine protection. Everyone knows that planking is a great exercise to build your abs, but if you want to strengthen your sides, exercises like the side plank will help work out your obliques. So, for day 15 of our 28-day wall Pilates challenge, we will be doing oblique training.

Step 1

You need to stand with your back facing the wall. Next, place your palm under your left shoulder. What is the position of your feet? Staggered. Your right hand should face upwards, pointing at the ceiling while lifting your hips.

Step 2

Now you must draw your arm down until it is under your upper body. Keep drawing it down till it can touch the wall behind you. You can lift your hips slightly while doing this.

Step 3

As you touch the wall, open back to a plank position while extending your right arm. Ensure that the fingertips of your right arm reach toward the ceiling. You can go for ten repetitions and then switch to your other side.

For beginners, reduce the reps and lift your hips higher when reaching for the wall. If your arms are giving out because of the pressure from the floor, you can place a soft material under your palm to make it easier.

Quadruped Leg Extension

This is an excellent exercise for beginners who wish to target their gluteus maximus while working out. It allows the practitioner to work out each side of their body independently. Unlike squats and lunges, which require a range of motion, the leg extension workout can be done with little to no range of motion. So, this exercise is the perfect alternative if you struggle to do squats or lunges. Here is how to do a Quadruped Leg Extension:

Step 1

Get on your hands and knees while facing the wall. Keep your wrists firmly placed on the floor. Under your shoulders is where you should position your hips and knees.

Step 2

When doing this exercise, it is essential to keep a flat back so that your cores will be engaged. Your arm should be lifted until it is equal to your shoulder. Your palm should be pressed against the wall while you pull your right shoulder blade back. It would help if you were far away enough from the wall so that your arms could be fully extended.

Step 3

Next, gradually stretch your left leg until it is fully stretched out behind your body. It would help if you extended your legs until your toes were pointing forward. Keep your pelvis level and raise your left leg until it equals your hips. Keep your left leg lowered so your toes are at least two inches above ground level.

If this exercise, as described in the steps above, is too strenuous for you, don't raise your legs to your hips level. Instead, raise it only to the point where you are comfortable. Remember that the arm you placed on the wall is there to aid as a support, and placing it firmly on the wall is one way to make this exercise much more manageable.

Triceps Push-Up With Side Leg Lift

As the name suggests, the tricep push-up with a side leg lift is a wall Pilates exercise designed to work out your triceps. The side leg lifts are designed to work out your thighs and glutes. This exercise is highly beneficial because it works out multiple muscles simultaneously. Now that we know what this exercise is all about and how it can benefit you let's get right into it!

Step 1

Your left side should be facing the wall as you stand with your feet together. Continue by crossing your left arm over your chest. Next, place your palm firmly on the wall. Like in the *Quadruped Leg Extension* exercise, you must stand as far away from the wall as possible while doing the tricep push-up with a side leg lift.

Step 2

Do you know how a clock hand works? Great! Now, slowly lower your left leg down the wall, imitating the movement of a clock hand. Move your left leg till it reaches the 9 o'clock angle of a clock hand before slowly raising it back to the starting position.

Step 3

Repeat the same movement using your right leg, but move the right leg to a 3 o'clock position this time. Keep alternating between your legs until the reps are completed.

If you struggle with this exercise, move your butt three to six inches away from the wall. Doing this will allow your legs to move quickly. If you wish to make the exercise harder, you can wrap an elastic band around your left foot. It would help to hold both ends of the band around your right hip for added resistance.

Day 17

Wall Knee Press

The wall knee press exercise will improve your overall posture, strength, and flexibility. This exercise also promises to tone your quads, upper back, arms, and legs. Your body core also gets stronger through this exercise. This exercise is beginner friendly. Want to jump into doing this exercise? Follow our simple steps below.

Step 1

Lie on your mat and place your butt on the wall. Your knees should be bent. Next, plant your feet about two to three feet up the wall.

Step 2

Gently raise your lower hips. Overlap your left knee and right ankle—keep your body in place.

Step 3

In a pulse-like manner, move your knees towards the wall ten to twenty times. Repeat the exercise by crossing your left ankle over your right knee.

For beginners, the pulsing can be done with your butt on the floor.

The Climb

The wall climb is another exercise that is excellent for improving flexibility. This exercise helps to work out the biceps, lats, calves, and core. The wall climb exercise can work out all these muscles because of the various movements involved.

Step 1

Face the wall and enter into a plank position.

Step 2

Put your right hand first, then your left, on the wall. Then, raise your hands to the wall as though you were "climbing" it. If you feel any pain or sudden pulls in your muscle, stop.

Step 3

Keep in mind that your arms need to be kept parallel while you are performing this exercise. Hold your position before moving your hands down the wall. Repeat the wall climb about ten times.

Beginners can make this exercise easier by staying closer to the wall. If you feel any pain during the exercise, it is a good idea to stop. The purpose of the exercise is to make you feel your muscles burn; it isn't intended to put you in any pain.

Day 18

Standing Crossover Crunch

The standing crossover crunch helps you to improve your range of motion and balance. It is also known to increase stability. This exercise works out the front abdominal muscles and makes you feel more tucked around your tummy. If you desire a tighter midsection, this is the exercise for you.

Step 1

Go to your wall and stand perpendicular to it.

Step 2

Place your hand on the wall and push one of your legs far away from the wall.

Step 3

Next, place the fingertips of the hand not on the wall behind your ears as you prepare to do the standing crossover crunch.

Step 4

Now you need to bend at the hips and draw the knee of the adjacent elbow together. The aim of drawing your elbow and knee is to get them to connect. Finally, return to your opening position and switch to the other side.

To make this exercise easier, don't kick your knee too high. Instead, draw it only halfway. Yes, your knees won't come close to touching your elbow, which is the point of the exercise, but you'd hopefully increase your range of motion as you practice.

Wall Leg Circles

Wall leg circles are exercises that target and strengthen your hip muscles. Examples of muscles targeted in the hips include flexors, abductors, and glutes. When muscles such as abductors and hips are strengthened, your balance will significantly be improved. This exercise is also known to improve flexibility which can reduce the risk of injury, especially in athletes.

Step 1

First, lie on your mat with your back and ensure your butt is in contact with the wall. Your legs should be kept extended up the wall.

Step 2

Your hands should be placed by your side while the lower part of your back is pressed into the floor.

Step 3

For the third step, ensure your legs are together and kept straight. Next, begin to move your legs in a circular motion. Start with small circles and then increase the wideness of the circles.

Step 4

You can make a circular motion for a particular set of reps. Alternatively, you can set a time. For example, you can do the circles for ten reps or 2 minutes.

Step 5

The direction of the circles should be reversed, and the same number of reps or time-set should be performed.

If this exercise is too strenuous, don't press your lower back into the floor too hard. You can also keep the reps low or reduce the time you set. Your legs should be kept straight and not touching the wall when doing the circles.

Day 19

Wall Angel

This exercise has often been called the V or W stretch. It is so named because of the position of your arms when you begin and end the exercise. This is an excellent exercise if you are the kind of person that sits behind a desk all day. The purpose of the wall in this exercise is to keep your spine in a neutral position. The wall angel exercises stretch your muscles, making your muscles more flexible and counteracting the effects of muscle-shortening exercises such as bench presses.

Step 1

Your feet should be about 8 inches away from the wall when you start this exercise. Your head, back, and butt should also be resented against the wall.

Step 2

Your spine position when you begin should be neutral. You can allow your spine to go neutral by moving your belly button towards your spine. A small drawing of your belly button should do the trick.

Step 3

Allow the back of your head to touch the wall by tucking your chin in slightly. If the back of your head is having difficulty touching the wall, place a pillow at the back.

Step 4

Now lift your arms until they are straight up and overhead. Your aim is to get the back of your hands touching the wall and forming a V shape. If the alignment is difficult for you, step your feet further away from the wall, and your alignment will become better.

Step 5

Start bending your elbows as your hands slide down the wall above your shoulders. As you slide your hands down the wall, ensure that your butt, back, and head are firmly on the wall.

Step 6

Maintain a good posture and slide your hands down as far as possible. You may feel a stretch, but you should not feel any pain. When your hands reach the lowest point, hold them in that position for a five seconds count and return to the V position.

Step 7

Do this exercise for ten reps, and if your muscles can no longer hold the V position without pain, it's time to stop.

If you have difficulty positioning your spine on the wall without pain, you can perform this exercise in a doorway rather than a wall.

Day 20

Wall Hamstrings Stretch

Chapter 6

Days 21-25

f you have wholly followed our 28-Day-Wall Pilates-Challenge up till now, congratulations, you have successfully passed the halfway point. Follow us as we take you through days 21-25. Are you ready? Let's go.

Day 21

Wall Push-Up

Wall push-up exercise is an excellent way to improve your stability while strengthening your muscles. If you struggle to do push-ups on the ground, you can try doing them on the wall. Your biceps and triceps are worked out during this exercise. This exercise also strengthens your upper body.

Step 1

Your feet should be kept wide apart while standing arm's length away from the wall.

Step 2

Proceed to place the palm of your hands on the wall and remember to keep them at a shoulder-level height. Your fingers should not be pointing at the ceiling. Move closer to the wall if your reach is too far.

Step 3

Bend your elbows slowly and lean your body into the wall. This is similar to how you tilt your body toward the ground when doing a regular push-up. Do not raise or bend your back; instead, keep your back straight and your elbows bent at a 45 degrees angle. Lean your body to the wall until your nose is almost touching the wall.

Step 4

Push back to your starting position. By maintaining a neutral spine during the workout, you can make it easier.

Also, your hips should not dip forward.

Day 22

Close Hand Wall Push-up

The close-hand wall push is a more challenging variation of the wall push-up. Instead of keeping your hand wide apart, for the close-hand wall push-up, your hands will be moved towards the midline of your body. Your palms will be kept in a diamond position. This exercise will place more emphasis on your triceps and pectorals. So, I wanted to give you a step up from the day 21 exercise, and here you have it; close-hand wall push-up.

Step 1

Your starting position should be where your feet and legs are kept close together. The appropriate standing distance from the wall should be arm's length. At shoulder height level, place your palms on the wall. Unlike the standard wall push-up, your palms should be touching each other.

Step 2

Keep your elbows tucked at your side, and bend your elbows as you lean into the wall. Keep leaning into the wall until your nose is almost touching it. Do not sag your hips, and don't bend your back. Keep your back straight.

Step 3

Repeat this exercise after you have pushed back to the starting position.

If this exercise is challenging, revert to the basic wall push-up.

Day 23

Wall Plank

The wall plank is an exercise for stability and posture improvement. This exercise also strengthens your body and primarily focuses on the back and shoulders. We can't also forget to mention that the wall plank makes your abs well-chiseled and defined. Your hips, butt, and pelvis are not left out when you do the wall plank.

Step 1

Choose your wall and stand facing it. Keep your feet hip-width apart. At shoulder height is the position where your hands should rest.

Step 2

Take a few steps backward while you are keeping your body in a straight line. You must get this part because the benefits of planking exercises come from how well your body is streamlined. Keep your hands on the wall.

Step 3

Now is the time to engage your core muscles as you press your hands into the wall. Ensure that your elbows are kept slightly bent. The position described in this step should be held for a few seconds.

Step 4

Your neck should be kept in a neutral position, and your body should be straight. Slowly step back into your starting position.

If you find this exercise difficult to carry out, don't hold your position for too long. Planking has always been challenging, so reducing the time you hold your position is okay. You can also place a soft material under your elbows if pressing against the wall hurts you. Keep your hips level as you engage your core muscles. Also, don't arch your back, and don't round your shoulders.

Day 24

Wall Side Plank

If you are big on strengthening your core and overall stability, the wall side plank is the way to go. This exercise dramatically improves your balance and stability while working on your abdominals. The wall side wall plank is a great glute and lower back exercise. If you want great-looking abs, you can't go wrong with this wall Pilates exercise.

Step 1

Pick a wall and stand next to it.

Step 2

Place your forearm against the wall while you keep your elbow beneath your shoulder.

Step 3

Now you need to step your feet away from the wall gently. This would cause your body to enter into a slight angle. The weight of your body should be supported by the side of your foot and your forearm.

Step 4

It is time to engage your core as your hips are lifted from the ground. A straight line from your head to your heels will be formed by lifting your hips.

Step 5

You will need to hold your position for some seconds before you lower your hips. Repeat this exercise for the other side of your body by turning around and placing your other forearm on the wall. Your aim is to hold each side of your position in the side plank position for 20 or 30 seconds.

Beginners can reduce the difficulty of this exercise by holding for ten seconds and moving closer to the wall. However, beginners should not move too close to the wall, or the benefits of the exercise will be lost.

Day 25

Wall Teaser

The teaser exercise helps you to improve your flexibility, control, and balance. If you wish to have a flatter tummy, this exercise can help you achieve that. The teaser is also a terrific exercise for increasing the mobility of your spine.

Step 1

Just like the other exercises in this book, the wall teaser requires that you stand facing the wall.

Step 2

Proceed to place your palm on the wall. Ensure that your palms are at least shoulder-width apart.

Step 3

Your body should be at a 45 degrees angle with the wall when you move your feet back. Your arms should become fully extended too.

Step 4

Proceed to brace your core and lower your body towards the wall as you bend your elbow. Push yourself back to the starting position and repeat for at least ten reps.

This exercise will be easier for you if you keep your body in a straight line. Also, ensure your cores are engaged and prevent your lower back from arching.

Chapter 7

Days 26-28

Yaaay! Just a few days left, and we will have successfully taken you through a 28 Days Wall Pilates Workout Challenge! It's been, indeed, an invigorating ride. Come on, tiger, let's push through the last four days.

Day 26

Wall Crunch

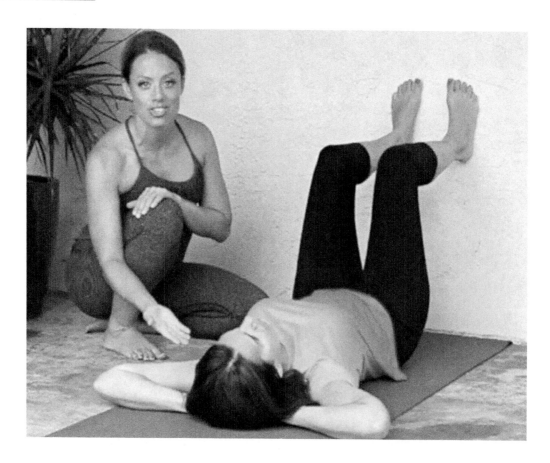

The wall crunch is an exercise that builds strength and endurance in your abs. It can also help slim down your waist while targeting the abdominal walls. If for some reason, you can't do abdominal crunches, you can try the wall crunch.

Step 1

Start lying on your back, keeping your glutes close to the wall. Proceed to place your hands behind your head.

Step 2

Next, extend your legs up the wall, lift your shoulders, and squeeze your abs. You can hold your position for a few seconds before returning to the starting position. Keep repeating this wall Pilates exercise till you are fatigued.

If the exercise is a bit challenging for you, use the hands you placed behind your head to push your head for support. Pushing your head from behind slightly will give your body a more accessible lift. You can also reduce the number of reps.

Day 27

Wall Knee Tuck

The wall knee tuck is similar to the standing knee tuck. The only difference between both exercises is that you use a wall in one. This exercise targets the muscles in your back and abdominals. Your internal and external obliques are also worked out when you engage this muscle.

Step 1

Stand facing a wall.

Step 2

Proceed to place your palms flat against the wall. Your arms should be kept at shoulder height, and they should extend out in front of your body.

Step 3

Lift your right knee as you engage your abs. Your knee should be brought very close to your chest as you lift it. It also should be close enough to the wall as possible.

Step 4

Hold your leg uplifted and slowly bring it back to the floor.

Step 5

Repeat the up and down movement for ten reps, then repeat for your next leg.

If you have a physical disability that doesn't allow you to lift your knee very high, you can raise your knee to waist level instead. You can also place your palms more firmly against the wall to act as better support.

<u>Day 28</u>

<u>Wall Bicycle Crunches</u>

Welcome to the final round of the 28-Day Wall Workout Challenge.

Whether trying to improve your core strength or have those chiseled abs you've always wanted, the wall bicycle crunches are your best bet. This exercise engages your entire core, which also includes your obliques. Spinal mobility is also an added advantage for those who engage in this exercise.

Step 1

Lie down on your back and extend your legs up, and empty the wall space.

Step 2

Your hands should be placed behind your head. Next, lift your shoulders, head, and neck off the ground.

Step 3

As you lift your body off the ground, bend your right knee and bring it close to your chest. You have to twist your torso so that it touches your elbow to your right knee.

Step 4

Next, straighten your right knee back up the wall and repeat the exercise for your left knee. Keep alternating each side, emulating the motion of riding a bicycle.

If you are a beginner and this exercise seems to be straining your neck, focus on controlling your movements. Please don't rush the reps; take it slow and steady. Even if you can only get out five reps on each side, it's better than rushing it and straining your neck.